TJ CLEMONS

Pimp Game

206

Don't Get Ready

Stay

Ready

TJ Clemons

itbftr@yahoo.com

Introduction

I used to get into trouble time to time growing up as a street kid.

It took me some time to slow down and look at what was important.

Me and my friends were very mischievous and we did crazy things.

I remember one time we decided to pull the fire alarm at school

because we found it amusing to have the power to have the men

from the fire department show up after we pulled the fire alarm.

We were walking down the street laughing afterwards, but then

somebody from school told on us for doing it, and we ended up

getting locked up for it. It was my first time getting in any trouble.

My mother had to come pick me up from the local police station.

And when I got home she wore my behind out with a leather belt.

I really didn't learn any lesson from it other than to not get caught.

I got into some more serious trouble when I was a teenager and

I ended up doing 6 months in a juvenile detention center for getting

caught again doing dumb things with those same friends from before.

Now that I think about it, we could have escaped if we really wanted to.

It was more of a psychological kind of incarceration more than it was

physical. Because we weren't really locked up inside of the building.

It was more like a boarding house for young guys like me and my

childhood friends. There wasn't even an actual fence around it.

The doors were locked, but we could have escaped from there anytime

that we wanted to. The problem was that there wasn't really any place

for us to go to after we escaped. And our parents would have found out

that we were missing from the boarding house and been looking for us.

And that would have only created a new set of problems for us and

our parents. So, we pretty much just stuck it out and made the best of

those six months the best way that we knew how to at the time.

I remember coming back to school the next year and all of the little

girls in my school started looking at all of us different.

Even the popular girls started giving me and my friends some play.

That bad boy image definitely elevated our status with the young

ladies, and I fully took advantage of it every chance that I got to do it.

They weren't just kissing us anymore. They started going all the way.

I got my first piece of action a few days in after the new school year.

All the girls seemed to want to get with all of us from then on out.

And we pretty much had our pick of the litter after we came back

to what we knew at that time as our reality.

It was a whole new world full of new and exciting sexual experiences.

And I really enjoyed all of the new attention and action I was getting.

That period of incarceration was due to burglary charges that me and

my friends had been charged with.

We were addicted to doing a lot of stupid things back then.

We didn't want to work for anything. So, we just started stealing things.

It was a stupid thing to do. And I wouldn't recommend that anybody

else get involved with those king of illegal activities, especially children.

We didn't even make a lot of money off of the stolen property.

It was basically the thrill of doing something illegal that motivated us

to go out there and commit petty crimes. Kids like us were just out

there running wild through the neighborhood and the city streets

looking for something stupid to get into.

6 months was a very long time to be away from home as a child.

It's a long time now, especially with all the responsibilities that I have.

I had missed part of two schools years and a whole summer locked up.

But that's where I picked up a lot of information about wanting to

start pimping when I got out of there.

A lot of guys my age wanted to be pimps when we grew up in the hood.

It was basically part of the street culture in our neighborhood.

We looked up to drug dealers and pimps because they were basically

the only guys who had a pocket full of money to flash to females.

And they had all of the beautiful women chasing after them.

Those were basically the only options that looked good to us growing

up around poverty. Because most of our parents were just barely

making it at their low paying jobs. So, we looked up to the hustlers.

They already knew how to handle themselves navigating the streets.

And we were very eager to follow in their footsteps when we could.

I remember trying to ask pimps questions whenever I got a chance to

while not trying to be annoying or in their way as a child.

This was my dream career and what I wanted to be when I grew up.

And most of the time they would tell me a few slick words here and

there. And it was just enough to keep me coming back for more

information when those opportunities presented themselves.

I met and talked to a lot of interesting pimps along the way. And all of

the information that they gave me sunk into my head and into my brain

and planted my first seeds into the game that would eventually grow

and get gardened and tended to until something amazing finally

sprouted into my first dose of reality in the game.

I knew that I wanted to pimp. And I was going to find a way to do it.

It was way different in the beginning because I was green as fuck.

I had no idea what I was doing at all until I started getting seasoned.

From those humble beginnings I became the man that I am today.

I started officially in the game at age 17.

 I had fallen in love with my girlfriend and she broke my heart.

We already had a baby together and I thought we were going to have

a family, get married, and live happily ever afterwards.

And after that situation I made up my mind to not catch anymore

feelings for another female on that deep of a level ever again.

I was going to be a player and play the field.

So, I started going after the promiscuous young ladies.

And eventually we figure out together that this was the foundation

for a very prosperous and profitable business plan after we put our

minds and bodies together and made some beautiful music together.

It was pretty much our ghetto version of a business plan.

It started off slow but eventually I got some more game.

Getting my heart broken really made me look at women different.

And that pretty much gave me the idea, motivation, and plan to make

things happen on in a very different way and on a very different level.

That mindset made me the perfect individual to start off pimping.

It turned a little bit of game into a whole lot of game over a lifetime.

I was always fascinated by the pimp and player lifestyle.

The pimps and prostitutes made the tracks a strolls look stylish.

They were dressed like they were basically at a fashion show daily.

And to a ghetto kid like me looking up to them that was everything.

I remember my first turnout. I can't even believe how it happened.

And then 6 months later we pulled her best friend into the game.

That's when I knew that this game was for me. I fell in love with it.

And that's also when I found out that I couldn't tell my friends about it.

None of the other guys that I had grown up with were pimping.

They were too busy running the streets and going back and forth to jail.

I had a few that I thought that I could possibly talk to about it.

But they couldn't even begin to understand the game that I was in.

Only me and my girls could have our own personal understanding.

If you stay ready, then you don't have to get ready!

I never believed in treating my girls badly or putting my hands on them.

If I have to do all of that, then I don't really need them around me.

I consider myself to be a professional gentleman of leisure.

I got in the game as a very young man and it was everything that I was

looking for and imagined that it would actually be like.

I love everything about the game and I remember when I fell in love

with game like it was yesterday. I remember parking my car on the

stroll and watching my girls do their thing.

I use to work 3 or 4 tracks daily to make my ends meet.

I got with one of the other players and we toured the country together.

I was always a really nice dresser but the game made me elevate.

If you looked good and dressed well women are naturally attracted to

a man with a good sense of fashion and style.

It instantly catches their eyes and their attention when they see us.

That little wheel starts rolling around in their heads.

They associate a well-dressed man with power, wealth, and success.

This begins the process of natural intrigue and attraction.

And they want to find out how they can associate themselves with you.

I remember admiring a lot of pimps and wanting to be just like them.

One particular pimp I looked up to had 10 women in his stable, that

included 2 sets of twins. That mother fucker was pimping hard as fuck.

I respected him so much that I talked about him all the time around my

girls, which ended up being a big mistake because he knocked a few of

my ladies after I did. And he snatched them up from right up under me.

I promoted him way too much and I learned a valuable lesson from it.

That whole situation knocked the wind right out of my fucking sails.

It hurt me real bad at the time but I eventually got over it.

It's part of the game. Me looking up to him, cost me a few women.

A lot of pimps don't like to talk about it. It's a cold-blooded feeling.

But eventually I got over it and I learned a very valuble lesson.

I ended up going on the road after that. And I picked up some new

female recruits along the way going city to city.

I was six women deep at the time. But I probably went through 50

women to be able to get those six women to work together smoothly.

All of those women don't end up staying with you for various reasons.

You have to deal with a lot of different personalities that don't always

get along together. It's basically a trial and error process.

You run into different mental issues and challenges along the way.

And you have to really get to know your women to become successful.

It gets complicated sometimes but that is all part of knowing,

understanding, and being there for all of them in your own special way.

Because if you can't handle your position as a human resource

manager, then your employees are going to run around wild, untamed,

and out of your control. And the next pimp is going to be sitting there

picking them off one by one, if his game is any better than yours.

Game recognizes game and you really have to tighten up your game

when the situation calls for it.

Luckily I was around a mother fucker who had mastered the game.

So, I sat back and let him do his thing while I soaked up all of his game.

His game was so tight, that I couldn't help but to get gamed up daily.

I knew one guy who was 30 deep with women.

And I didn't let any of my girls be around him anywhere in his presence.

He could have knocked one on my ladies with eye contact alone.

I wasn't going to take any chances with them being around him.

My pimp partner showed me the game of taking my girls on the road.

He had already been around and he knew all of the major prostitution

tracks and strolls from coast to coast.

 I learned a lot coming up under him including how to dress to impress.

I remember one track that was only 3 blocks long.

But 90 girls worked those 3 blocks and you had to have the pick of the

litter if you wanted to make some real money with being surrounded by

all of that competition. Our girls learned to step their game up though.

That friendly competition created a very different level of respect and

communal brotherly love for each other amongst a chosen few pimps.

I started to stick out like a sore thumb when my game stepped up.

I wanted to be a major player in the game until I caught a case.

I ended up doing a little time and I came back ten times stronger.

I learned a lot while I was away on my all-expense paid state vacation.

I did the crime and my time, and I came back even more motivated.

I wrote a book about my life story while I was away from society.

I needed something to inspire me to come home to. Because I took a

very dark turn because my mother passed away while I was there.

The guards thought I was working on my case and asked me why I

was always writing something every time they passed by my cell.

One of the guards actually recommended that I started typing my book

in the law library. And that's basically how this book came to be.

I don't personally care for drug usage with me or with my girls.

But just about any pimp who believes that their girls are totally clean

is a fool who has a bag of magic beans somewhere in his household.

He probably keeps that kind of information to himself to avoid

drug dealers from approaching his women and having them follow

after him like the pied piper from those childhood fairy tales.

At least one of your women are addicted and hooked onto something.

You can't fool or lie to yourself as a pimp because it happens.

You can try and fool everybody else but sooner or later they find out.

In my mind you want to try to uplift them and try to get them off of it.

But that is a very different beast that has a mentality of its own.

You can only do so much. And a habit can change everything.

Most of the time it's not for the better, and if that's what they want to

do then eventually they will move on and continue to chase their high.

Women who are on drugs are a lot harder to manage because their

drugs control them and their entire thinking process better than you.

Every pimp goes through this situation at one time or another.

My childhood was magnificent.

My mother and father both had decent paying jobs and they both tried

to spoil me to the best of their abilities. I had all the finest things.

Both of my parents drove new automobiles straight off of the lot.

I was a pretty smart kid who learned to pay attention to details.

They didn't really care for me getting into the pimp game at all.

They both wanted me to settle down in the square world and get a job.

They never ever understood that pimping was a career for me.

It's my chosen profession. And I studied the game to get good at it.

They also didn't understand that it took hard work and dedication for

me to elevate in the game. So, that one day I could eventually become

a top notch player getting respect in the streets for what I was doing.

It didn't happen overnight. I really had to put some work into it.

My parents still supported me in everything that I did along the way.

But they didn't really want this lifestyle for me.

I had already made my mind up that this is what I really wanted to do.

And I worked my way up in the game year after mother fucking year

until I had almost four decades up under my belt.

I was determined to pimp or die. And pimp until I died.

I felt like the black sheep of my family sometimes.

But I did what I had to do to make all of them love and respect me.

Some of my younger family members looked up to me like a king.

And a lot of them wanted to be just like me when they grew up.

They couldn't keep their eyes off of the beautiful and exotic women

that I brought to several family functions. That was to be expected.

I actually had to take a break from pimping for a while, because I had

two children with one of my girls and she ended up taking off on me

and leaving them behind for me to take care of.

It took a little while to adjust to that situation but I got back to it when

I got things figured out and situated with my children.

I did everything for my kids. I took them to school every day.

And I made sure that they had the best of everything growing up.

So, I had to learn all of the aspects of the game, while in the process

of also becoming the best father that I could for my kids as well.

Love is more important than money because you can always find ways

to make money. And you have to find the right woman to fall in love.

I had a whole lot of women over the years and I loved them all.

If a woman goes out there and brings you back money she loves you.

She took all of those risks out on the tracks, streets, and strolls for me.

They put their lives in danger every day selling their bodies for me.

That's a very loyal and dedicated woman if you ask a pimp like me.

And if you don't love that woman with everything inside of yourself,

then something is obviously mentally wrong with you.

I do everything in my power to do everything that I can for my women.

There is no such thing as a 401 k in this game.

So, I give all of my women a daily allowance and I put money away for

them, in the process of taking care all of their other daily needs as well.

Every 30 days I buy my women some kind of jewelry for their loyalty.

The longer that they are with me the more expensive jewelry they get.

And I save up money for them for when and if they want to retire.

I have never even heard of another pimp doing all of this for their girls.

I build my women up and provide them with a future when they get out

of the game working with me as their financial manager.

The life expectancy of a female working in this game is only 5 years.

So, if you're able to keep a woman with you for over 5 years you're

really doing something special especially if you're letting them out

of the game with enough money to retire from it and do well.

If she is running around, in and out pursuing different aspects of the

game over a long period of time ,it becomes a very dangerous lifestyle.

I used to hold hands and pray with my girls every day before they went

went to work, because I was raised in the church.

And I wanted the arms of protection from God himself around all of

them every single day while they were out there in the streets for me.

And I made sure all of my girls took self-defense classes as well.

I wanted them to be able to get out of any hurt, harm, and danger and

come home to me after they put in all of the work for my organization.

Some of these tricks try prostitutes. And my girls were ready for it.

They beat up a few guys really bad. But they had it coming.

They shouldn't have been putting their dirty hands on my property.

God doesn't like ugly. And they got themselves some instant karma.

My whole style is very different from the average pimp in many ways.

I grew up in the old days and I distinctly remember a lot of the old

sayings. And the main one that I heard from a lot of the old folks and

the pimps was:

You have to stay ready so that you don't have to get ready!

And you don't have to be scared if you're already prepared!

Most pimps are different and we are extra ordinary individuals.

We were created to manage our women efficiently and effectively.

They have to understand our philosophy and the ways that we think.

We are giving the game to them daily, so that they understand all of

complications, hindrances, and stumbling blocks that come their way

can be handled better if they follow our commands, instructions,

strategic planning, and blueprints to the best of their ability.

That is what pimping is all about. That's why we are there for them.

Pimping is a job, a career and, a profession. We are all mortal men.

It's all about the attitude of that man that makes him a good pimp.

You can't be mean, brutal, and violent to your women.

That is going to only bring you more problems that you don't want.

This is a gentleman's game. And I play it hands off without contact.

I'm not going to go through all of that toxic bull shit and drama.

If a mother fucker beat my ass every single night before they went to

sleep, then that mother fucker probably wouldn't wake up one day.

And a woman is going to feel the exact same way in violent situations.

You have to really treat everybody including all of your women the

way that you would wanted to be treated in that exact same situation.

Some women have actually killed their pimps and got away with it.

Self-defense is pretty much a get out of jail free card right then.

You have to remember that we're living in the human trafficking era.

And females are still considered to be the weaker physical sex.

So, don't set yourself up for failure from a jail or a death sentence.

A lot of men under estimate their women, but brain strength can

over power physical supremacy any day, especially when a woman

automatically recognizes that the legal system is already on her side.

Pimping is what we do but you have remember that you're a man first.

You have to already know that you control her mind first, then once

that goal is accomplished. then everything else will fall into place.

You have to stay ready at all times, so that you don't have to get ready!

The game doesn't ever change, only the players in it.

The times have changed.

And just like in professional sports, it's a new season every year.

The women are still choosing their pimps to work with them.

They are choosing drug dealers and gang bangers instead of pimps.

These kinds of guys don't know or understand the pimping game.

That is where the actual problem lies in most cases.

They are choosing the wrong kinds of unprofessional men.

The same thing is basically going on in the square world.

These modern women are choosing the wrong types of guys.

Then they get upset with the results from their own choosing practices.

They are saying that these square mother fuckers and new age pimps

aren't qualified for the positions that they have openings for.

They try to make these square mother fuckers, drug dealers, and

gang bangers into something or someone who they really aren't.

These types of men aren't qualified for the game because they have no

idea what the fuck that they are doing. And they don't have any

understanding of what the game is even about in the first place.

You have to study the game from a real mother fucking pimp.

This isn't a temp agency position. You have to know what you're doing.

You just can't wake up one day and start pimping and expect some

kind of professionalism from a randomly chosen individual.

You have to come up under the pimping to know how to pimp.

These new guys don't want to learn how to pimp.

They want to ignore real pimping and not listen and learn anything.

This isn't always the case but it's what happens more often than not.

There are a few young guys doing their thing under the supervision

of real life street managers. I love to see when real pimping is going on.

It's a very fascinating and beautiful thing to see with your own eyes.

A lot of these new guys are creating their own style with gangster-ism

instead of actually following the rules and regulations of the game that

has been passed down from generation to generation for almost 200

plus years of real mother fucking pimping in America.

And drug dealers have stepped in and followed the same exact suit of

their gang banging partners. It's crazy when I see it going on.

And they have caused the federal government to come in and trump

up the regular pimping and pandering charges to these new human

trafficking charges which sometimes carries a life sentence.

We went from doing 6 to 18 months to doing up to 30 to 60 years.

The worse off that your previous criminal record is, the more time that

you're potentially going to be facing based on the severity of the

criminal charges that you have been indicted on for human trafficking.

Just because these guys are getting pimp cases doesn't mean that they

are actually even pimps. Every man that gets money from a woman

isn't a pimp. There is a very clear difference in making real pimp moves.

Just a few a months ago I pulled into a gas station on the local stroll.

Three men with guns attempted to rob me at gunpoint.

The police patrolling the stroll pulled right in the same gas station.

All three of them were known to the vice squad as pimps.

Instead of asking me to help them get gamed up and learn about

becoming better street mangers, they caught some robbery charges.

Back in my day when didn't move like that. We used our brains more.

When we saw a man dressed like me we tried to learn from him.

I could have provided the young guys with some real street knowledge.

I would have been willing to mentor them so that they could elevate.

It's just a different overall mentality.

We respected the game a lot more.

This isn't a part time or temporary position. You have to be all in to win.

These new drug dealing and gang banging pimps are basically throwing

rocks at the penitentiary, trying to break a window to get into it.

I see these so called pimps drag racing on the track.

They are chasing women down every time they come back with money.

You have to move with a lot less intent to commit illegal crimes.

And it is really giving the pimp game a black eye.

Real street hustlers and pimps move in silence.

These mother fuckers are advertising and showing their hands way too

easily. These mother fuckers are basically in the way of real pimps.

They are messing up royally and glorifying stupidity at an all-time high.

These drug dealers and gang bangers don't know how to act like real

gentlemen that know how to follow our basic rules and regulations.

They don't have the proper communication skills to be real pimps.

They want to rob real players like me, instead of finding out all of the

valuable information that a mother fucker like me can give them

on so many intricate and diverse levels.

They want instant gratification when the game needs to studied daily.

It's a scientific process of learning how to pimp at the highest level.

Even the average mother fucker in the square world goes to the experts

in the field of whatever they want to do as a career. And when they

graduate they go out into the square world in search and entry level

position to start off in their new professional careers.

And when they get more and more knowledge then they get

promoted to a higher position until they eventually get into a lower,

middle, and upper level management position in their chosen field of

study as part of their business or organization.

That is basically how it works in the square world and in our universe.

You don't just jump into the game and know everything.

You move around in it and pick up little pieces of it everywhere you go.

You travel around the country on different soils, tracks, and strolls.

You keep doing it over and over again daily until the student eventually

becomes the master. You get more and more seasoned every day.

And you and everybody else in the game spread and sprinkle all of

game around and until you're seasoned enough to cook a 4 course

meal for all of your women to be able to eat off of every single day.

This whole world is actually set up for everybody to win.

You just have to know how to be able to read the blueprint.

And sometimes it just comes with age and experience.

You have to learn how to come correct in this game to become

successful at it. There aren't any shortcuts or any other ways around

putting work into your game in order to elevate in this mother fucker.

It's a dirty game that we are out here playing every single day.

You have to be able to get down in it and get your hands dirty if you

seriously want to make some real money as a financial manager.

The level of game that you have mastered is basically your resume.

Your reputation is based on the amount of work that you put in daily.

And the women who chose to be with you are your references.

I'm still addicted to the game. It motivates me to elevate in it.

I need the game as much as the game needs me to be in it.

My relationship with the game is solid, eternal, and ever-lasting!

These new guys are still jealous of the men like me with real game.

They try to rob us and run us out of town because they know that a

real mother fucker with knowledge and information about the game

can easily pull their women from right up under them.

These young ladies are instantly attracted to the qualities that

gentlemen like me naturally possess. And they are drawn to it like a

very powerful magnetic force to metal.

These young ladies entering the game now are tired of getting knocked

over the head, punched in the face, and kicked in their asses because

most women want to be treated like queens, especially if they are

handling their business, selling their bodies for you, and putting their

hard-earned money in your pockets. And these young guys just aren't

able to grasp that simple concept for whatever reason that may be.

It's basic game to me. The average woman wants to be romanced.

And they also want to be honored, respected, and appreciated for

everything that she is doing for you in advancement of the game.

It's not Chinese arithmetic. It's a basic mathematical concept.

You get out of her what you're working hard to put in her mindset.

If you keep putting your foot in her ass then sooner or later she is

going to put her best foot forward and walk right out of your life.

Like the old folks used to always tell me:

You're going to catch a lot more flies with honey.

And they were mostly right most of the time.

I was young and foolish but eventually I got tired of bumping my head.

As I got more older and experienced, I ended up getting a whole lot

less headaches, when I learned to listen, learn, and apply all of that

information, wisdom, knowledge, and understanding to what was

actually going on in the world around me into real-life situations.

I had to learn the game both inside out and outside in.

A lot of different people taught me a lot of different things.

You have to be open to listening and learning if you want to advance,

accelerate, and elevate in this game if you want to win in it more

often than not. You're constantly applying life lessons to life situations.

That is exactly how you learn how to thrive and survive in this game.

Dumb mother fuckers end up in dumb situations.

That's just how the fuck it is. And that's just how it's going to be.

I didn't make the blueprint. I just learned how to read and follow it.

People like me with longevity in the game know exactly what the fuck

that I'm talking about because we have watched mother fuckers enter

and exit the game in a million different ways based on their mindset,

mentality, and survival instincts.

You never know what to expect to happen. All you can really do is

learn how to expect the unexpected. You don't always have time to

get ready when something suddenly happens. So, you have to already

be prepared and ready for unexpected things to happen daily.

These streets are just like the jungle.

They are full of predators and prey.

Any individual can take on the role of the predator and the prey and

any given moment instantly right before your mother fucking eyes.

Any time money is involved or part of the equation, then you must be

on guard at all times. Because at any given moment in time a hungry

predator is lying in wait to jump out of the cut and pounce on you

in order to take your women, your money, or your life.

It's a very realistic daily outcome and expectation.

We walk around playing the dominant role fully knowing that other

mother fuckers have jealousy, envy, and hatred for us existing very

deeply within their hearts and minds. It's just simply part of the game.

The natural selection process is always in effect.

It is embedded and engrained deeply into our street life and culture.

We have to remain mindful of all of the reality going on around us.

And some of us in the game just don't possess those survival skills.

None of us are invincible or immortal but we can increase our

awareness exponentially and remain mindful of the people, places, and

things that we choose to surround ourselves with at all times.

And you have to always stay ready, because you don't always have

time to get ready. A few seconds or a few inches can often determine

if you survive a situation that may be introduced to you in an instant.

This is the lifestyle, occupation, and environment that we chose for

ourselves and to be around. And we live and die by those choices daily.

Anything can happen instantly. Your whole life situation can change.

I advise that you treat people with honor and respect at all times.

Take good care of the people that take care of you, especially your

women because they can easily become your Achilles' heel.

They can bring you down faster than you could ever imagine.

A woman scorned is one of the most dangerous weapons known to us.

Only a man who doesn't love himself mistreats the woman

(or in some cases the women) who love him.

If you choose to play with fire then you might just get easily burned.

It's like a jungle sometimes out here and you have to do your best from

going under against all mother fucking odds while you're in the game.

The average female in the prostitution game makes $400 a day.

There are a lot more women making a lot less money.

And there are a lot less women making more than the average.

And the average stripper only makes about $2000 a month.

While most strippers only bring home about 2 to $300 a night.

This is the point that I'm basically trying to make.

There are regular escorts and then there are super whores.

Super whores are just naturally created and they are about their

business when it comes to participating in the game because they

are naturally motivated to outshine their competition.

Instead of pulling in a few hundred dollars they make a few thousand.

If you're making at least $1200 a day, then you fall into that category.

From what I know and to have come to understand about this lifestyle,

it would be more advantageous to just legalize prostitution.

It needs to be placed inside of a controlled and concentrated area.

The only place that I know that actually does this in the United States

is in certain areas in the great state of Nevada.

If we had buildings and secured facilities where we could do this legally,

then it would tremendously cut down the crime, violence, and murders

perpetrated against all of the women working in the sex trade.

Once these big shots and millionaires figure out a way for the

government to collect taxes on illicit acts across the board, then they

are going to jump on board and make it a reality.

That's pretty much how it's going to work. Because America is very

greedy when it comes to taxes and fees that they aren't actually doing

anything to generate all of that cold hard cash money.

Ten years ago you didn't have to pay taxes on anything that you

purchased on the internet. And now they are collecting trillions of

dollars for not doing much of anything other than making it possible

through legislation. I'm looking forward to seeing it happen because it's

only a matter of time before more and more women turn to

prostitution as a career.

50 percent of these young girls dream about growing up to be

escorts, porn stars, and strippers. Some of them are only motivated

enough to make money off of social media sites like OnlyFans.

It's part of the culture and it will continue to be.

A lot of the young bitches don't want to work at a job.

Most of them don't have any other natural skills or abilities.

All they want to do is jump on their knees and spread their legs.

Listen to the sexualized music that they listen to.

It's all about being a good for nothing lazy whore.

I didn't invent the wheel. I just learned how to use it to my advantage.

I learned how to dress, rest, and ride. And I got good at it.

And I got better at it along the way until I mastered the game.

Pimps are one of the most hated and hated on members of society.

There are many different kinds and types of pimps.

The word pimp only describes their title in their relationship.

It's pretty much these new guys giving men with this title such a bad

reputation because of all the bull shit that they are doing in the name

of pimping. And they are using their criminal cases to create mass

hysteria across the whole mother fucking country.

All you hear about pimps in the media are that they are kidnapping

underage women and forcing them into prostitution against their will.

That does realistically happen about ten percent of the time.

But the 90 percent of the guys who are not doing those things are now

automatically being classified as human traffickers.

That's why the laws are like they are now.

And that's why pimps are being viewed as evil mother fuckers.

Most pimps aren't bad guys. I'm pretty sure that some are.

But the majority of us are upstanding members in our communities.

We help a lot of women get out of bad situations.

And in return we get set up by the legal system and demonized.

They arrest women on minor charges and get them to make up

horrible stories in exchange for dropped or reduced charges.

In some cases they incentivize them with housing programs.

They will give them free room and board for years and years.

All they have to do is point the finger and the mother fucker that was

there for them for years and years. Then they get rewarded with all

kinds of government funded assistance.

I have seen this happen to a few of my old partners with my own eyes.

It's a cold mother fucking game. And it's getting colder every day.

A lot of the women that get into the game have been molested by

either their close family members or their foster families, or both.

Those kinds of women are often weak and vulnerable because they

were forced to endure and survive through the worse kinds of

violence and abuse imaginable.

They have been through a lot. And they can more easily adapt to pretty

much everything that goes on inside of the game.

And every female isn't usually built like that.

And a very high percentage of women come from those kinds of

backgrounds or similar kinds of circumstances.

Their mothers were on welfare or drugs and made bad decisions.

And they grew up in an environment of poverty, despair, and

desperation that they want to escape the generational curses that they

were conceived, born, and bred into.

Most of their mothers chose drug addiction and their men over them.

It's a vicious cycle of destruction generation after generation.

And it will repeat itself until someone breaks that barrier into a better

a better overall situation and circumstance within that mentality.

I met the families of a lot of the girls working with me.

And once they actually got to know and understand me and all of my

philosophies, and knowing how their daughters were before they met

me, they actually gave me their blessings and support.

I made that much of an impact in the lives of my women.

And they actually started building relationships with the children that

they left behind for their families to raise. We even started giving them

"child support" to help with all the expenses of raising their kids.

I believe in karma and doing the right thing for the right people.

I went to prison but it changed me for the better.

I took on a totally different outlook on life and became a better version

of myself that I am very proud of today. It's part of the game.

Sometimes we catch cases but it's for us to learn valuable life lessons.

Some people look at it negatively. I look at it as a blessing.

It may have actually saved my life. I do know that it happened for a

very specific reason. So, I decided to use it for positive reasons.

I got to sit back and take a real good look at my life and everybody

that is in it. And I decided then and there to be the best version of

myself that I could possibly be. I'm very far from being perfect.

But I am a very good person and an example of humility.

I learned to humble myself. And to really look at everybody's

circumstances and life situations before I automatically judged or

dismissed them.

I give everyone the opportunity to come to me on a deeper human

level. I'm very compassionate and understanding of most people unless

they try to run some kind of bull shit game on me.

I have been in different types of situations where I wanted people to do

that exact same thing for me and I was openly denied.

 That's a very hurtful and demeaning personal experience.

Sometimes you have to give a person that opportunity to do so.

But so many people lose it by not just coming correct in an open

and honest manner that the average person deems to be

respectable. It realistically doesn't always happen that way.

But at the end of the day it is a very personal choice to live by.

 All those guys that beat their women and force them to sell their

bodies against their will bring that karma directly back of themselves

double fold. And they deserve everything that is coming their way for

misrepresenting the pimp game.

I am a very religious man. You couldn't change your life if you wanted

to because everything that happens is already written.

I am a pimp because I was supposed to be a pimp.

God is using me he way he wanted me to be used.

There is lots of drama and chaos in the life that I lead.

But this is the life that I chose and I am able to overcome all odds.

I was fortunate to be blessed in the game for a very long time.

I only had one girl who worked with me that passed away.

She was messing with a guy in the mafia.

It had nothing to do with what we were doing together in the game.

She was dating a guy involved with that lifestyle.

Some kind of way she owed somebody a large amount of money.

They wouldn't even accept the money that I offered them in exchange.

They wanted to take her life instead. I don't know all of the details.

But it's a very dangerous lifestyle for women to be in.

They often get targeted by serial killers and sick mother fuckers.

These killers come in and do real damage to females in the game.

It's a tragedy that you really don't hear the details about sometimes.

It's a very dangerous lifestyle to be tangled up into.

So, many things happen to these women that really need to be talked

about and addressed on so many different levels of conversation.

If you have something better to do with your life then find a better

occupation to get involved with. I have your best interest in mind.

I'm just giving you the real and raw information straight from my

heart, mind, and soul. I love my women and want nothing but the

best things in life for them, and their families, and children.

Try something different if the opportunity presents itself.

Get your education and make something happen for yourself.

I'm a mentor, money manger, and psychologist amongst other things.

I made love to my women and I also put my religious doctrines and

philosophies inside of them. I basically did everything for my girls.

I was the husband to many wives. I treated them right according to

the rules and regulations of the game.

A lot of pimps get murdered while they are in the game.

It's a very dangerous career for us to be in as well.

I had a girl affiliated with gang bangers get something started.

Nobody was messing with her or anything of that nature.

She just felt some kind of way for some kind of reason.

I had left and went on about my fucking business that day.

And she ended up getting some guys shot originating from that

particular altercation. She just felt some energy and showed her

ability to start some shit out of the thin mother fucking air.

Some people are just seduced by the power that they have in that

moment and they don't really care about the consequences of the

people or the lives involved.

And they are ready, able, and willing to make some ill shit happen at

the drop of a mother fucking dime. And we have to simply adjust our

personal situations to adapt to that kinds of bull shit when it comes

into play which is basically on a daily basis.

That's just the world that we reside in now.

Pimps get murdered by tricks as well.

Those kind of things happen and they really need to be addressed.

It's a dangerous lifestyle for us as well because of the jealousy, hatred,

and envy that other men have for us.

I actually had very strong romantic feeling for all of the women that

chose to be with me. It was a very humbling experience being in the

game that I am grateful to be associated with for a lifetime.

My women trusted and believed me on a deeper level.

They allowed me to put their lives in my hands.

And I never failed them. I always came through for them.

It fascinated and exited me. And I made a whole lot of money.

And I have learned to look at life as sheer greatness.

I never get depressed because I stay ready and motivated.

Every day we are going to go through struggles.

Every single day somebody is going to test you.

Somebody is going to put you through a series of tests.

It may be human beings. Or it may be God himself.

I feel like the King James Version of the bible is watered down.

It was orchestrated and designed to control the minds of the masses.

They don't really want people to think for themselves.

So, they put a leader in front of them to guide them into the direction

that the powers that be want them to go. And there really isn't that

much difference between preaching and pimping.

It's basically the exact same thing. Pimps and preachers both provide

their followers with their philosophies about life and how it should be

lived according to their doctrine and concept. And they both charge a

fee for their services. And a lot of preachers sleep with various women

in their congregation whether or not he is married or living the

single life.

It really doesn't matter because they are naturally attracted to the man

in the leadership position. And they are always showing off their

feminine attributes to charm their way into his good grace.

They show off their bodies, cook him meals, and even try to contribute

large amounts of money to try to get his undivided attention.

The preacher just uses "Church Game" on the women who

are more religious-minded. But it's all about that all mighty dollar bill

at the end of the day. Because he wants to basically live that same

luxurious lifestyle as a mother fucking pimp.

I grew up in the church and I recognize all off the various techniques

that these men of God use to solicit money from their congregations.

Nobody even knows what the original scriptures even said in them.

They have been translated and passed down from generation to

generation and whoever is in charge at any given moment in time is

going to make it fit their own ways of thinking. They are naturally going

to use as much power and influence that they have at that particular

moment in time to benefit them in as many ways possible as they can

with the main objective being financially beneficial to themselves.

It was created to simply pacify and control as many people as they

possibly can. And most of the people who fall into that category are

the female worshipers. Their minds are often able to be manipulated

more easily because by nature most women are delusional in some

way, shape, or form. And they are usually the object of sexual intrigue.

And just like in the pimp game these religious leaders also know and

understand that once you have the ability to control her mindset and

her thought process, then you will more easily have control over her

body and at that point and time it belongs to you sexually as well.

These religious leaders isolate us and then spoon feed us their ways of

thinking using the same basic concepts that are often incorporated in

Pyramid and Ponzi Schemes. They give us the illusion of religious

freedom and expression, while in the process of shaping and molding

what they want our mindsets and thought processes to adapt to.

And they create a social concept of classifying their members into

falling in the financial classification of the haves and the have not's.

They set up a scenario in which they enlist most of their followers

from higher class backgrounds so that they can seek like-minded

individuals like themselves to join into the religious audience to

become paying members who also financially support this tax-free

alleged non-profit religious organization.

It's a religious hustle in my personal opinion. And it always will be.

It's the whole purpose and design of this version of a tax exempt

corporate for profit organization.

Religion is a great way to isolate and separate like-minded individuals.

And when you separate people from each other then it creates

confusion and mistrust of people who don't think exactly like you do.

And it makes it that much easier to manipulate them mentally as well

as financially. Anything can realistically be going on behind those

closed doors when that kind of brainwashing is going on.

If we all treated each other with dignity and respect it would change

a lot of things for the better.

We live is a very segregated and separate society where people are

programmed not to get along with each other based on their different

kinds of beliefs, cultures, and religions.

We need to start treating people better instead of looking at them like

they are our adversaries and enemies just because they have a

different way of thinking and articulating their religious freedom

of expression. People only act the way that they are taught to.

And having a different religious concept should not change or

affect how they are treated by other members of society.

We tend to think that we can build our own destiny and fate alone.

But it often takes the help and assistance from all kind of people from

all different types of races, cultures, and religions.

I live in one of the better parts of town around well to do people.

And I bet every single one of them has some skeleton in their closets.

They have done something that they're not proud of at some point

along the way in their lives. But hopefully they picked themselves up,

dusted themselves off, and turned their lives around for the better.

Some people are only viewed as being bad people because somewhere

along the way they got labeled and classified as a bad individuals.

Pimps like myself often fall into this category.

These people pointing their fingers at me often don't know anything

about me other than I'm in associated the pimping game.

They can't say or point out a single thing that I have done wrong.

Yet they have made up their minds that I'm automatically a bad guy.

They don't have any information to support their claims whatsoever.

It's all based on rumors and innuendo instead of factual information.

God gave me enough wisdom to go my way and choose my own path.

And that path led me directly into the game.

 And I'm glad that I made that decision for myself every single day.

It doesn't matter what I do good or bad because I decided to choose

pimping as my profession and career and that automatically gets me

labeled as a bad guy from a social perspective alone.

These are labels that the people in our society decided that made

perfect sense to them at the time. And that way of thinking continues

to exist when it comes to our community standing.

And the average person just feels more comfortable trying to treat us

as unwanted outcasts until it comes to holding their hands out when

we spend our money in their business establishments.

That love of the all mighty dollar simply changes things in that moment.

And once we walk away that jealously, envy, and hatred for us

automatically turns back on like clockwork.

Some of these types of people really need to look at themselves and

inside of themselves and try to look at all people simply as human

beings in search of a better way of doing things in their journey.

People who judged other people will never make their own personal

jealousy, envy, and hatred of men like me ever make any sense at all.

All that we can do as a society is to continue to keep moving in the

right direction and learning from our own mistakes and bad decisions.

That's exactly what is wrong with people living in this era.

They are not willing to learn any information of substance.

This is the age of information where almost all knowledge is assessable.

They have a mass amount of technology at their fingertips.

Yet the masses simply choose to be ignorant of the factual evidence.

And they listen to the news and mass social media to get all of their

facts, figures, and statistics. And they repeat that same information

that is being spoon fed to them daily.

When they need to be listening to people like me who are constantly

trying to spread awareness, enlightenment, and all kinds of realness

that is actually based in reality.

A lot of people want to sit back and spread information that is actually

just their own opinions like it is factual. They sit back and make

themselves look like fools and I pretty much find it entertaining.

Most information can be found easily on the internet.

It doesn't take much time or effort at all.

And a lot of them try to look educated or enlightened by simply

repeating information that they hear about in news reports.

That is information that the news reporters read off of the script that

they are being paid a decent wage to dictate to the masses fluently.

This world is full of followers. We need more intelligent leaders instead

of people who blindly follow without trying to search for the facts.

People make all kinds of assumptions. But they never just ask what they

actually want to know about other people. And they just automatically

accept that I am a bad guy based on my profession as a pimp and

the norms of society. I can be a good or bad guy. It actually has nothing

to do with my career choice. It's actually based on my own personal

character and behavior pattern and how I choose to treat my women

and everybody else around me in my inner circle.

We are all both good and bad at different times.

None of us are perfect human beings.

We are simply a product of our upbringing and environment.

Every day we are different versions of ourselves based on our daily

interactions and experiences. We all have our ups and downs.

I try to be the best version of myself every single day.

But things happen. And we have to react to them accordingly.

It's basic human nature. And most of us are humane.

None of us are perfect. We all have at least one flaw.

We haven't been here before. And we have a lot of journeys to take.

And I am willing to learn something new every single day.

That's exactly why my mind has the ability to expand exponentially.

That is when and where wisdom happens.

I spend a lot of time by myself and I try to advance my thinking.

I love to learn life lessons. But a lot of people don't.

They walk blindingly into death and destruction daily.

You have to have that appetite for learning new things.

You have to feed your brain knowledge and wisdom daily.

It makes life that much more unique, interesting, and exciting!

You have to know how to think for yourself and react accordingly.

You can't just listen to everyone and digest their information.

You have to have the ability to seek your own knowledge and

understanding of the world around you to even have a chance to

be able to survive on a day to day basis.

You have to build up your character and your confidence.

You can't do what everybody else is doing because it's trendy.

You have to be a trend setter and blaze your own path.

Mostly everybody else is trying to fit into society.

I'm personally trying to set myself apart from everybody else.

The people who actually know me find me interesting and enlightening.

And the ones looking at me from the outside think I'm a villain.

But the only actual opinion of me that actually matters to me is

my very own. I live my life to impress myself and not others.

I'm my biggest critique and my best congratulator.

I don't pay much attention to negative energy because positive energy

brings positive results and vice versa. I'm naturally drawn to positivity.

The rest of that shit is for the fucking birds.

I don't really give a fuck about what people think or feel about me

because I don't entertain fuckery. I'm like Janet Jackson in that regard.

'What have you done for me lately?'

Probably nothing at all so you and your negative thoughts and opinions

can keep it moving accordingly and "Ease on down the street!"

I done give one, two, or three fucks about what they think about me.

If the world ended tomorrow I know that there is only one mother

fucker like me in this world who lived my life to the mother fucking

fullest no matter what people thought of me.

And I live my life freely.

I think for myself. And I do what I think is the best for me to do.

Fuck everything and everyone else.

I have my own spirituality and mindset.

My life is meaningful because I treat the people around me good.

It's not all about the money with me.

It's about me being the man that I want to be.

And it's about me being true to myself and true to what I believe in.

The people who really made an impact to me growing up were the

ones who had pride in themselves even though they were living in

poverty conditions and situations.

The men took care of their women and children.

And they worked hard every single mother fucking day to live better

than they did the day before until they put them and their families

into better overall conditions and situations.

They didn't just sit down and accept defeat.

They looked overwhelming odds in the face and took them on.

And eventually they lived decent lives with their families.

They had charisma, confidence, and self-respect for themselves.

They didn't drown in despair and sorrow.

I have been there before. I didn't always have money.

I slept on other people's couches, in cars, and outside sometimes.

That really doesn't mean shit unless you give up hope for yourself.

I could tell you where I have been.

But it's way more interesting to tell you where I'm going.

We all have been down. But you have to pick yourself up.

And dust yourself off and do what you can until you can do better.

And you have to learn how to stay away from mother fuckers with

that 'crab in a bucket mentality.' Those mother fuckers are way too

mother fucking happy in the company of misery.

Those mother fuckers don't even try to get out of the bucket.

They just sit back and try to pull mother fuckers back in with them.

We all have the power within ourselves to transform into a more

successful version of ourselves. We just have to have the confidence

and motivation to keep on keeping on when the going gets hard.

We all have that gift inside of us but some of us lose it along the way.

You have to learn how to go get it back sometimes.

That's what makes you stronger and more resistant to outside forces.

God made each and every one of us for a reason and a purpose.

And our life time is designed for us to find our place in the universe.

Do what make you happy in your own personal situation.

It is impossible to make everyone else around you happy all the time.

I had to learn these lessons and blessing for myself.

You have to do what you have to do sometimes.

Even your parents can lead you in the wrong direction.

You have your own thoughts, feelings, and ideas.

I'm very glad that I learned this on my own.

It really helped me out in the long run and made me who I am today.

I learned to agree to disagree and keep moving in my own direction.

I got everything that I have now from life experiences.

You may look exactly like your mother or father, but at the end of the

day you are your own individual self with your own concept of what

you want to do with your life choices and decisions.

You're born looking just like your parents.

But you die looking like all the decisions that you made for yourself.

It's not about how I chose to play around in this game.

It's about what I observed in the time that I have been in it.

You have to know how to deal with people, especially your women.

The times change daily. Technology changes daily.

We went from pagers and payphones to cell phones.

And now you can post your girls on the internet if you want to.

But you still have to live by certain values and codes in the game.

It was established by rules and mother fucking regulations.

It was created, setup, and structured for real mother fuckers to become

successful business entrepreneurs in the pimp game.

Now it's so cut and watered down that I barely recognize it anymore.

It's not about guys like me exploiting women at all.

It was intended to be a secret society that you had to get blessed into.

It was an honorable and respected lifestyle at one time.

We are supposed to be gentlemen of leisure.

You're supposed to be seen but not seen to the point where you bring

a lot of attention to yourself by beating your women and working with

underage little girls, or forcing females to sell themselves.

There is no honor as a man in any of these activities.

Cruelty to women isn't part of the game.

They are trying to used pimping as an excuse to be the type of man

that they already are and always wanted to be anyways.

That is not ok. It just makes the rest of us looked fucked up.

This game is meant to be free-spirited and mutually beneficial.

These females are supposed to choose to be with a mother fucker who

is going to make their overall situation and lifestyle better as the man in

their lives that brings them security and stability.

I'm here to tell my own personal story.

I'm the author, creator, editor, illustrator, publisher, and writer of it all.

Nobody can tell me a single thing about myself. I got this.

I operate on a very different professional level.

I stand up for me and my people.

I dress nice and treat mother fuckers the exact same way unless they

choose to come at me sideways or on some fuck shit.

Then I might move different to adjust to you accordingly.

It's these so-called high society mother fuckers in suits and ties that

you really have to worry about.

 Those of the real mother fucking villains!

They hide in offices and make fucked up rules to try and control us.

They want mother fucking followers that don't ask any questions.

And the find ways to tax us more and more until nothing is left over.

It's these politicians and business men that are fucking up society.

And they want to manipulate us daily with news reports.

I was created to help my community and the people around me.

I have no intentions of hurting anybody in this world.

I'm just the fall guy. And they use men like me as scapegoats.

They point the finger and send law enforcement after me.

When I'm just trying to make a living with my girls because we have

to feed our families. People are just uncomfortable with pimps,

prostitutes, and drug dealers because they don't think that we pay

taxes.

But in reality we pay just as much or more money in taxes.

We buy everything from nice homes to luxury automobiles.

So, we definitely pay our fair share of taxes.

The government is just greedy and corrupt and they want their hands in

everybody's pockets 24 hours a day 7 days a mother fucking week.

And they have the nerve to label me a mother fucking criminal.

They got tired of putting all these females away on misdemeanor

charges and started going after the men who patronized professional

women and the men that manage them properly and improperly.

It's all about commercializing criminal activity and collecting money.

They want to turn businessmen like me into their own personal slaves.

They literally hand out hundreds of years sentences for human

trafficking now so you really have to be on your toes in this game.

I'm on a very much respected level in this mother fucking game.

I'm not a tennis shoe pimp or a hoe hustler.

Tennis shoe pimping is a state of mind.

It's not necessarily what you choose to wear on your feet.

It's the way that you move around and live daily.

You usually aren't making any real money.

You're just trying to survive off of a female every single day.

It's just me looking from outside of the game looking inside from a

distance. And the things that I am seeing from my own personal

perspective is that a lot of these young guys are doing it because

it's in style. They are pretending to be pimps simply for clout.

They have no real intentions on elevating their game.

If you're going to do it then you might as well do it the right way.

Don't be playing with the pimping.

A woman can get dick from just about anywhere.

And some men simply have to pay if they want to get some pussy.

A woman can basically get it for free anytime she wants to.

That's where the knowledge and understanding comes into play.

Teach her how to sell her body correctly for a higher price.

It's simply supply and demand. You have the supply men want.

And they are willing to pay higher prices to gain access to it.

And once you have that mental control over her everything else

will fall into place under your control and authority.

It's the perfect business model.

You have to know how to mentally stimulate her.

She has to want to be down with you on a much different level.

She is your female partner in the game that you're playing together.

I fall in love every day with the life and the lifestyle that I am living.

I woke up this morning and I have a chance to upgrade myself.

Every single day is an opportunity to make something happen.

I have never been in love with a woman.

But I do love what we can do together and make happen together.

I give my girls my full attention and I put everything into them.

It's in the average female's nature to be fruitful and multiply.

You just have to know and understand how to use it to your advantage.

Be who you really are. Don't be a fake or a mother fucking snake.

This game isn't for these kinds of men for real.

The game will chew you up and spit your right the fuck out.

Because if they like you then they're going to fuck with you, but if you

cross the wrong female then she is going to send you up the river

without a mother fucking paddle.

(That's to prison if you can't keep up with me.)

Real love is spectacular. And it only happens a few times.

You really have to know how to play this game if you plan on winning.

Going different places really makes you into who you are.

And lot of these mother fuckers with college degrees bounce around

from job and never really find themselves or any kind of happiness.

But they want to talk bad about pimps like me who are very happy

and successful in our chosen profession and career path.

So, what did that all basically do for you?

Sometimes nothing at all. They spend their whole lives chasing a

dream or goal that they will never achieve. I'm not downing it or

talking bad about anybody it's just simply an observation.

My job has a lot of security because pussy will sell just about anywhere

and anytime 2 hours a day 7 days a mother fucking week.

What they really want to know is, how is somebody like me who

basically came from nothing doing much better than I'm doing?

I don't really have an answer. I'm just living my best life.

It burns a lot of mother fuckers way down deep inside though.

They have been watching me for years and years trying their very

best to figure me out. But they just don't fucking get it.

You have to stay ready so that you don't have to get ready!

It's that old school vibe and energy!

This whole world is actually set up for everybody to win. You just have

to be able to read the blueprint. And sometimes it comes with age and

experience.

This current financial crisis brought on by the United States government

is creating the perfect storm and climate for pimping and prostitution

to make a major comeback.

It is the oldest profession that dates back as far as biblical times.

Prostitution is also referred to in several books of the bible and in

several bible texts verses and stories.

Jesus Christ himself is linked directly to Mary Magdalene and several

other working women. He is also rumored to have been involved in

sexual relations with prostitutes. Jesus is even rumored to be

participating in the prostitution game as a pimp.

The devil represented as a serpent in the book of Genesis is often

compared to a pimp because he tricked Eve and controlled her mindset

to the extent where she would manipulate her own husband Adam into

doing his bidding which led to their predicament of getting evicted from

the Garden of Eden.

(Which basically makes Adam the first trick that ever existed.)

Prostitution is going to be the next thing and wave of new businesses

opportunities across the country. It is relatively inexpensive to open

and operate. And most women are already in the position to start up

their own franchise operations.

Human capital is basically the only resource required to make

everything possible with the assistance of a communication device and

access to wireless internet services.

This is going to become the next trending business model for startup

entrepreneurs looking to start their own local businesses and

corporations from their homes or the local motels.

Trust and believe the words that are coming out of my mouth.

Because a lot of women are about to put their pride to the side and

begin their journey into the world of making their money in an

innovative and creative way of doing something that has already been

going on since the beginning of time.

In just about every economic condition pussy will sell.

The price of that personal commodity is losing more and more value

daily. The average price on the streets is only about $40 dollars.

And it will adjust accordingly based on the scale of supply and demand.

You might not believe me now but you will see for yourself in the very

near future in American society.

Prepare yourself for the next chapter of business opportunities in our

free market environment and economy.

Pimping and prostitution is going to solve the financial problems of a

lot of people in our great country and our society as a whole.

I'm seasoned for a mother fucking reason.

I basically grew up in the game and with it along the way.

I was raised by the pimps hustlers and players in my neighborhood.

And the one major league pieces of information that acquired from

them was that pussy is a commodity that will always be available to buy

sell and trade on the open market all day every mother fucking day

long.

And it's a very profitable business to be involved with for any potential

entrepreneur who wants to start up their own corporation as an escort,

pimp, or prospective professional prostitute.

Its a very lucrative industry that has very low startup costs.

And it also relatively easy to promote on the internet.

The profit margins are astronomical compared to just about any other

traditional career path that a woman with no training, education, or

trade skills could possibly pursue for themselves.

You can't just be a regular human being to be involved in this game.

You have to be an extra ordinary individual with integrity intelligence

and charisma.

This game creates articulate and imaginative street chief financial and

executive officers that know how to run their businesses efficiently and

effectively.

I am playing chess out here while other mother fuckers are playing

checkers. I can see their moves coming from a mile away. It's almost

insulting.

But I also have learned to accept their limited knowledge,

understanding and thought processes. It is my strength and their

weaknesses.

One thing that I learned from the life experience is that the people

closest to you that actually need you the most will cross you in a

moment's notice.

They are constantly trying and testing you in order to find your

weaknesses, while they are putting their plots and plans against you in

motion daily.

One example from the bible was Sampson and Delilah. She kept trying to figure how to destroy him using her sexuality. Eventually Sampson let his guard down and Delilah got him caught up in her tangled web of deception.

This is very much like a pimp and prostitute relationship.

 These bitches may appear to be loyal on the outside but inside their heads they can be using that feminine mindset to fuck up everything in your life at a moment's notice. It's just in their nature to do so.

Also anyone else that you're around may also be envious and jealous of

what you have going on. And they also have seeds of deception and

destruction growing in their mental gardens.

People are watching every move that you make and every step that you

take. And my personal advice to you would be to always stay focused

and ready so that you don't have to get ready when these mother

fuckers put their plots and plans together in motion against you.

You don't have time to prepare for war because every day you're out

there on the battlefield of life.

So, keep your eyes and ears open at all times and be prepared for the

bull shit because it's already clear and present and ready for you daily.

Stay ready at all mother fucking times because you don't always have

time to get ready. Because you're putting your life on the line every

single mother fucking day whether or not that you have come to

that realization or not.